YOUR KNOWLEDGE HAS VALUE

- We will publish your bachelor's and master's thesis, essays and papers

- Your own eBook and book - sold worldwide in all relevant shops

- Earn money with each sale

Upload your text at www.GRIN.com
and publish for free

Bibliographic information published by the German National Library:

The German National Library lists this publication in the National Bibliography; detailed bibliographic data are available on the Internet at http://dnb.dnb.de .

This book is copyright material and must not be copied, reproduced, transferred, distributed, leased, licensed or publicly performed or used in any way except as specifically permitted in writing by the publishers, as allowed under the terms and conditions under which it was purchased or as strictly permitted by applicable copyright law. Any unauthorized distribution or use of this text may be a direct infringement of the author s and publisher s rights and those responsible may be liable in law accordingly.

Imprint:

Copyright © 2016 GRIN Verlag
Print and binding: Books on Demand GmbH, Norderstedt Germany
ISBN: 9783668620803

This book at GRIN:

https://www.grin.com/document/387743

Olga Piro

The End of Slave Trade in Egypt

GRIN Verlag

GRIN - Your knowledge has value

Since its foundation in 1998, GRIN has specialized in publishing academic texts by students, college teachers and other academics as e-book and printed book. The website www.grin.com is an ideal platform for presenting term papers, final papers, scientific essays, dissertations and specialist books.

Visit us on the internet:

http://www.grin.com/

http://www.facebook.com/grincom

http://www.twitter.com/grin_com

The end of slave trade in Egypt in the context of East Africa.

Keywords: XIX century, Egypt, end of slave trade, Sudan

Abstract: *In this paper I will discuss the slave trade boom in Egypt and Sudan at the middle of the XIX century and its following abolition by Egyptian government in 1873. Several legal attempt of abolishing Egyptian slavery were made along the XIX century, before the period of the Veiled Occupation (1882). It will be showed that the particular fact of a slave trade boom has to be connected with the increasing demand of cotton by the international market in the 1860s and this can explain the following decrease of the slave trade in less than twenty years.*

Introduction: In 1805 Mohammed 'Ali[1] took the power in Egypt following the orders of the Ottoman Empire rulers. In the following years, he took Sudan (excepted Darfur) under his control and introduced for the long staple cotton production in Egypt. Thanks to 'Ali's innovations, Egyptian economy became (and stayed for the whole XIXth Century) an economy centered on cotton production, whose trade was put under the State control. Egypt Historians, as Fage[2], traditionally analyze the features of the Egyptian cotton production as an output of European aim of penetrate the region, remarking that the new economic developments had been made possible by the penetration of British capitals in North Africa. In few words, from the 1820s to the 1870s, Egyptian economy was reshaped by the British and Ottoman dream of transforming it into an economy based on a low-cost cotton production. But this doesn't explain how Egypt could put together the work-force which was necessary for its new agricultural system. For this reason, different scholars, since the 1970s, tried to analyze the development of Egyptian economy in the run of the XIXth Century from the development of its own workers class. The fundamental works on this topics are those by Gabriel Baer[3], O'Fahey[4], Ralph Austen[5], all remarking the important role played by the slave trade from Sudan in this context. This paper will concentrate on the final part of this story, namely on the legal abolition of slavery and slave trade in Egypt in the years 1873-1877. How could these legal measures become effective? It will be argued that their efficacy depends on the increase of the cost of buying slaves.

---

1   Mohammed 'Ali was an Albanian commander sent by the rulers of Ottoman Empire in 1805 with the task of challenging the former (and bad) administration of the Mamelukes in Egypt. He finally killed his adversaries in a Borgian way ,but he was later fought and defeated by the Ottomans in 1835. He planned to expand his power to Sudan arriving even to Lake Victoria in Ethiopia, at the aim to organize the whole area as a Nile-centered land economy. He entered into Sudan in the 1820s and exploited the conquered territories stealing gold and slaves, imposing a high taxation and using all these resources for the building of new infrastructures in Egypt. XIXth Century Sudan was not a united territory under one State power, as Egypt already was, but it hosted two different great sultanates, the Darfur and the Funji, both Muslims and slave traders.
2   See mainly J. D. Fage and R. Olivier (eds.), "The Cambridge History of Africa," Cambridge UP
3   Gabriel Baer explores the social impact of the XIXth century slave trade in Egypt, highlighting its importance.
4   Author of texts which analyzes Darfur and Sudan, such as "Darfur Sultanate" for Oxford university press
5   Ralph A. Austen, "The 19th century Islamic Slave Trade from East Africa (Swahili and Red Sea Coasts): A Tentative Census", University of Chicago Published online: 13 Jun 2008.

We will also compare the Egyptian experience and the Sudanese one. The largest part of the actual Sudan[6], was under Ottoman-Egyptian rule at that time and it had the same legal obligations of the Egyptian territories. The Mahdist revolution[7] (1881-1898) interrupted the Ottoman rule on Sudan, increasing the internal use of slaves. The later British-Egyptian administration of Sudan (called Condominium, 1898-1956) could not eliminate slavery in Sudan as well. In 1923 Great Britain protested because Ethiopia, entering in the League of Nations, had on its territory people subject to slavery. Some voices pointed out, against British position, that in Sudan the situation was pretty much the same[8].

The importance of the slavery in the XIXth Century Egypt can be hardly over-estimated. The peak of the slave imports from Sudan to Egypt has verified between 1860 and 1867 with 10.000 slaves imported yearly. But, only then years later, the law against slave trade was promulgated (1873) and the legal condition of slavery was abolished (1877). A clandestine import of slaves continued for many years, but with very reduced quantities [9].

The trade route (see chart 1) through which the highest amount of slaves was traded into Egypt, was called "the Forty days route". The prices of slaves are reported in Table 1 In 1837 a British Pound corresponded to 100 Egyptian piasters.[10]

Table 1	
Year	Black Male in CAIRO
1800	185-340 piastres
1813	230-280 piastres
1837	800-900 piastres
1840	636 piastres
1845	848 piastres
1850	1038 piastres
1877	1000-2000 piastres

[11]

---

6   With the exception of Darfur, which was conquered in 1874. Darfur was an independent Sultanate and its main source of income was slave trade. It is very likely that the aim of ending slave trade, by British, could have been strengthened by geopolitical considerations about cutting revenues of independent territories such as Darfur was.

7   Mahdi revolution was an Islamist revolution guided by a figure called Mahdi, who fought against foreign rule in the country with an eschatological propaganda who associated the fighting against the Evil with the Prophet Jesus. The Mahdi conquered Sudan and established his power in Khartoum between 1881 and 1885. When the English-Egyptian troops conquered Khartoum in 1885, the Mahdi died. However, his successors had the control on other parts of Sudan, being defeated only in 1898. In the Chart 1 it is possible to see the maximal extension of Madhya (1882-1885).

8   "Slavery in the Twentieth Century: the evolution of a global problem", Suzanne Miers, 2003

9   Estimated around 500 people yearly

10   Reda Mowafi "Slavery, Slave Trade and Abolition Attempts in Egypt and the Sudan 1820-1882", Lund Studies in international History 14, &ESSELTESTUDIUM, 1981

11   Reda Mowafi "Slavery, Slave Trade and Abolition Attempts in Egypt and the Sudan 1820-1882", Lund Studies in international History 14, &ESSELTESTUDIUM, 1981

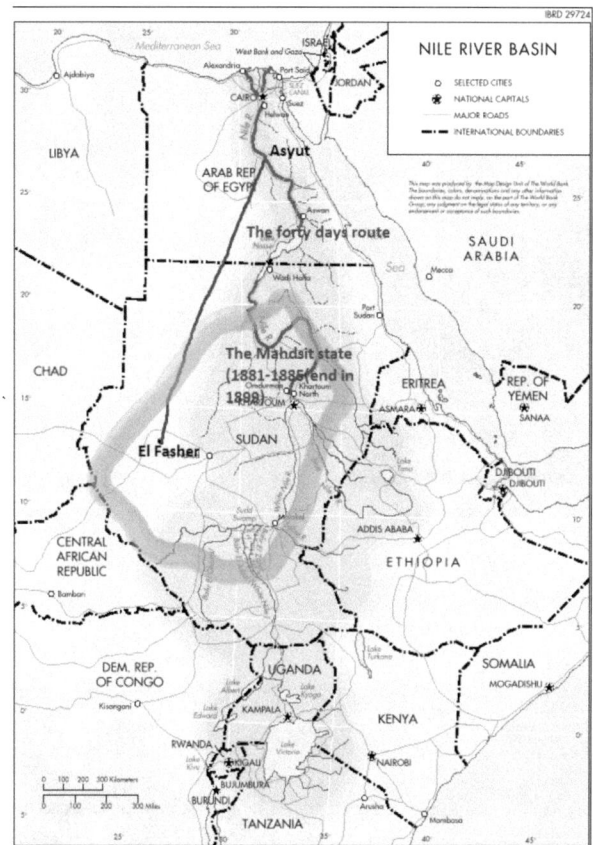

Chart 1:
the forty days route (Darb el Arbain), which connected El Fasher to Asyut on the Nile. The Mahdist state (1881-1885) interrupted the furniture

Source: https://712c6c1c-a-62cb3a1a-s-sites.googlegroups.com/site/eraselahistoria/home/1o-eso-ciencias-sociales/las-culturas-de-asia-anterior-mesopotamia-the-egyptian-civilization/the-egyptian-civilization/nilebasin.gif?attachauth=ANoY7cpX7KQH0uRjeEs9P16dg4Jqn9 3nco2LQVO9mYlKsJzj0ScIKl7ru5hZCP1zCJOHHFUTljy-aXuoZJE11HsxM0_7GrB23bnixsy41VirvKAwU3a9IYtiHXHQ3s4ezpwY_0DY

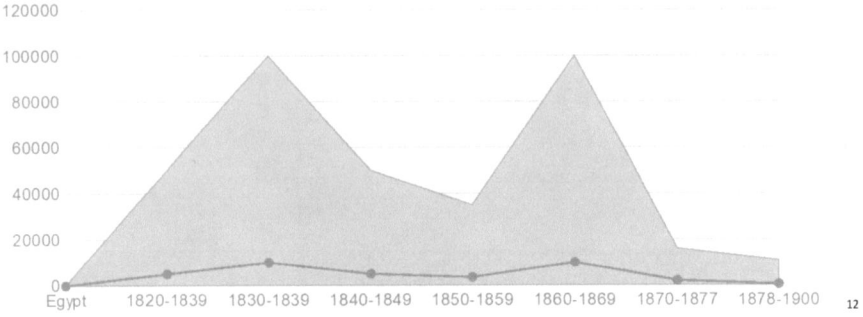

Graph 1: Slave imports in Egypt (blue line) and overall number of slaves living in Egypt (green)

The Egyptian necessity of workforce: cotton production in Egypt

Table 2 – Cotton production in Egypt

Year	Average Crop (ginned cotton)
1850-1859	687
1860-1869	250,743
1870-1879	469,356
1880-1889	576,133
1890-1899	1,061,187

In 1838 a treaty between Great Britain and Ottoman Empire created the possibility, for the British subjects, to send capitals in Egypt[14]. On monetary side, the Egyptian currency reform in 1835, gave to Egypt a bimetallic standard and allowed the following growth of banking activity since 1850s, improved by the invention of telegraph. These new measures gave to Egyptian governors the capitals[15] which were necessary to modernize Egypt, financing the perennial irrigation in Nile Delta and cultivated long-staple cotton, sugarcane and rice (and finally the Suez Canal). [16]

---

12   Data in table 1 are from: Reda Mowafi "Slavery, Slave Trade and Abolition Attempts in Egypt and the Sudan 1820-1882", Lund Studies in international History 14, &ESSELTESTUDIUM, 1981
13   Data in Table 2 are from Cotton in Egypt, Read P. Dunn, JR. Director of Foreign Trade, National Cotton Council of America 1948
14   The treaty, applied in 1842 in Egypt, made possible to send British capitals in Ottoman Empire.
15   Tariq M. Yousef, "Egypt's growth performance under economic liberalism: a reassessment with new GDP estimates 1886–1945" Georgetown University, Washington, D.C, 2002. The fact that capital investments and cotton trade deeply linked Egypt and Great Britain, can be proved by the study of Yousef. He provides evidences of a long-term equilibrium between UK and Egyptian monetary values, evidencing the prices' convergence between the two countries.
16   Despite the high growth rate, Egyptian government started since 1858 to be strangled by foreign debts.

The integration with world trade is reflected by the Egyptian trade balance. 1823 imports counted for 656,000 English Pounds, exports for 1,455,000 E Pounds. In 1838, the total value of trade increased to 3.5 million E Pounds, in 1850 to 3.7 million E Pounds, in 1880 to 21.8 million E Pounds (moreover, Egyptian trade measures are officially stated to be undervalued until 1911). [17] Between 1838 and 1865 cotton export increased 10.5 times in volume and 21 in value. The introduction of the Ashmouni cotton gave also a boost in production in Upper Egypt, due to the development of a perennial irrigation system. [18] (Table 2)

The last boom of foreign demand was notably due to American Civil War. In these years (1861-1865), the cotton area grew from 200'000 to 500'000 acres. After the war, the cotton price started a decline which would continue until 1900.

The growth could probably have been still higher, if Egypt would not have been affected by workforce scarcity. The harsh treatment (expropriation, forced labor and high taxation) reserved by government to *fellahin*, made them flee to Palestine between 1830s and 1840s. Moreover, at the starting of XIX century, mortality rate was very high. The end of wars and the rise in nutrition and life standard brought to an increase in birthrate along the XIXth Century, but this change became important only in the last part of the century, as we can see through Table 3.

The population growth in Egypt and the end of Slavery

Table 3 Year	Population of Egypt	wages compared in % of Great Britain
1846	4,476,439	
1860	5,506,253	
1882	7,840,271	11.90%
1897	9,734,405	13.80%

[19]

The large increase of Egyptian population during the XIX century (table 3) was due to a higher quantity of food, to the regime stability and a lower mortality rate with respect to the former years. [20] The Napoleonic war and the poor administration of Mamelukes had made Egypt a country with few million people in the 1810/1820s. Since 1830s until 1880s, the country needed workforce of every kind in order of actuating those land intensive cultivation plans, which 'Ali had planned and started and the Ottomans had pursued after him. One of the responses to this difficulty was the slave import. Another response was the use of forced labor by

17   Charles Issawi "De-Industrialization and Re-Industrialization in the Middle East since 1800", International Journal of Middle East Studies, Vol. 12, No.
18   P. Dunn, JR "Cotton in Egypt",. Director of Foreign Trade, National Cotton Council of America 1948
19   Data on wages are from Jeffrey G. Williamson, "Real Wages and Relative Factor Prices in the Third World 1820-1940: The Mediterranean Basin", Harvard University Discussion Paper Number 1842 July 1998. Data on Population are from Justin A. McCarthy, "Nineteenth-Century Egyptian Population", Middle Eastern Studies, Vol. 12, No. 3, Special Issue on the Middle Eastern Economy, 1976
20   McCarthy, "Nineteenth-Century Egyptian Population", Middle Eastern Studies, Vol. 12, No. 3, Special Issue on the Middle Eastern Economy, 1976. He evidence in the years 1800-1846 the deep impact of plagues such as pestilence and Cholera and the Mohammed'Ali's wars on the Egyptian population in urban and rural areas.

fellahin[21], which was important in the construction of infrastructures such as Suez Canal.[22] As the scholar Henry Verhoeven suggested, the growth in slave import was the natural outcome of both the will of Ottoman Empire and Great Britain. The Empire needed a growth in tax revenue[23] from Egypt and Great Britain needed cheap cotton. In fact, Egyptian cotton was absorbed mainly by Great Britain (at the 80% in 1900)[24].

How could this dependence on slavery be broken? There were different events, all happening at a same time. On one side, the British Empire and the Egyptian governors wanted to apply a Western development model to Egypt, using consequently salaried workers and not slaves. This trend of legal abolition of slavery is common to all the countries which were under the British sphere of influence even if, as I anticipated, its enforcement was not always attended. Another important fact was surely the Mahdi revolution in Sudan, which impeded the use of the Forty Days Route since 1881.

But, probably, the most efficacious element in the elimination of slavery was the decreasing cost of the free workforce, a decrease due mainly to the effects of the population growth. Since the 1870s, wages were at 11.90% and in 1890 their annual growth was at -0.21.[25] The negative growth of salaries suggests a very low demand of workforce compared with its increasing quantity. A free worker earning from 5 to 10 piastre each month was an incentive to abolish slavery.[26] Moreover, at that time, the cost of a slave amounted to 1000-2000 piastre and this was not an incentive for slaves demand. Finally, the free workers protection was almost inexistent at that time but the mortality on workplaces was high. Even this can have made more risky the investment of buying a slave than that of hiring a free worker.[27]

Now, one must consider that the cotton production had become less profitable after the end of the Civil War in the USA (1865), but that Egyptian cotton producers decided to go ahead with the cotton production even if a lower prices. In these new conditions, all the reason for the choice of free workers hereby mentioned became very efficacious. Of course, one cannot point the risqué cost of buying a slave (compared to the cheaper salaries of a daily worker) as the only reason why slavery was abolished. The

---

21 *fellahin* means agricultural laborer, peasant
22 For the amount of *fellahin* utilized and their conditions, in the construction of Suez Canal, see Vladimir Borisovich Lutsky, "Modern History of Arab Countries", 1969
23 Considering that this project transformed Egypt into an indebted country, changing its role of tax contributor for Istanbul, one must be surprised by the lack of foresight of the leaders of the Ottoman Empire. But one must also remember that the whole Empire was going to fall.
24 Harry Verhoeven "Water, civilization and power in Sudan, the political economy of Military-Islamist State Building", African Studies, Cambridge University Press ,2015
25 Jeffrey G. Williamson, "Real Wages and Relative Factor Prices in the Third World 1820-1940: The Mediterranean Basin," Harvard University Discussion Paper Number 1842 July 1998
26 Zvi Yehuda Hershlag "Introduction to the Modern Economic History of the Middle East", Brill Archive, 1980
27 Tariq M. Yousef, "Egypt's growth performance under economic liberalism: a reassessment with new GDP estimates 1886–1945" Georgetown University, Washington, D.C, 2002"*The historical claim that income per capita improved little or not at all in the first half of the 20th century is supported by our results*". This condition is clearly related to the lack of improvement of wages of low-skilled workforce (see table 3)

abolition of slavery was also a form to give a form of "nobility" to the imperialist action of firstly Eguptian and then British forces in Sudan.

Since 1830s, slavery was increasingly denounced by the Europeans as an uncivil heritage of the past. Both France and in particularly Great Britain, during the XIX century, saw abolition as a central issue of their foreign relations with Egypt[28]. In Khartoum, however, the slave trade continued as normal, since the authority had very little control over the regions between the Nile and the Red Sea coast. It seemed necessary, since the 1860s, to penetrate till the lakes of Equator, principal sources of the Nile, to stop slave trade. This also gave a reason to the Egypt Government wish to extend its control over a region which was rich in water resources[29]. In the 1870s, Egypt was able finally to abolish really the slave trade from Sudan, thanks also to the fact that it took the control of Red Sea ports at the place of the Ottoman Empire. However, this would have been probably not enough without a scarcely perceptible but continuous change of mind toward slavery in the Egyptian society and, most of all, without the Mahdist revolution, which, after 1881, cut the roads, which made possible the arrival of the slaves[30].

Sudan and Slavery

The previous explanation of the sudden decrease of slavery in Egypt can be confirmed through the observation of Sudan. Darfur Sultanate, the only part of the actual Sudan which did resisted to British or Egyptian penetration, fell finally in 1874; according to Mahmood Mamdani, a Darfur historian,

It was the collapse of the royal monopoly over the slave trade that led to the collapse of the Sultanate, which came when the demand for slaves skyrocketed in the late eighteenth century with the incorporation of the region into the larger slave plantation economy. [31]

In Sudan, during the XIX century, each landowner normally owned from 20 to 200 slaves. There are no precise estimation of the number of slaves in the country but Mowafi, through an analogy with similar economies, estimates them as 20-30% of the whole population. The various nomadic tribes were composed by slaves from the 8% to the 40% of population; in the urban center slaves were about the 15.25%. In 1838 it is reported that 20000 slaves pro year, coming from Trans-Saharan and Nile valley, joined the Red Sea coast, the great pole of slave trade in North/East Africa. Another supplier of slaves was Abyssinia: in 1860s from Abyssinia to Darfur, arrived 18'000 slaves per annum. Then, 12'000-15'000 slaves were exported from the South of Darfur to Khartoum. Over 1,250,000 slaves were exported from Abyssinia to Darfur between 1800

---

[28]Reda Mowafi
[29] Harry Verhoeven, 2015
[30] Reda Mowafi
31   Mahmood Mamdani, "Saviors and Survivors : Darfur, Politics, and the War on Terror",   Three Rivers Press 2010.

and 1850. By 1876, also if diminished, the overall trade in slaves from Red Sea to Arabia was about 30'000 annually[32].

Sudan and the Arabic Gum production

Turkish administration established a centralized cultivation in Sudan and taxed it, at the goal of financing Egyptian transformation. The racial antagonism between tribes increased. [33] The Turkiyya started some irrigation processes in Kordofan, often with foreign technical support, which rose the production: the export of Arabic Gum amounted at 3000 quantars[34] of the early XIX to 20'000 quantars (900 tons) in the 1850s [35]. The Arabic Gum was the most important product of Sudanese economy and its market was liberalized in 1849, letting rise the Gum export from the 3000 quantars[36] of the early XIX century to the 20'000 quantars (900 tons) in the 1850s. With the reconquer of Khartoum (1891), Ottoman government decided to boost the export of Arabic Gum, from the 2'000 tons of 1891 to the 11,816 from the only Kordofan in 1904.[37] At the end of XIX century, foreign workforce arrived from Chad [38] and Niger and became the class of *fellata*. These people populated the Oriental and Northern Sudan and worked in cultivations. After the Mahdist parenthesis, Sudan fell under the rule of a joint British and Egyptian rule, from 1898 to 1956. The British were, as we saw, one of the world's political antagonists of the slavery. Nevertheless, the way in which the country was developed left outside of the patterns of modernization a the high majority of the country, instead focusing only on single industries as cotton[39]. No wonder that, in spaces outside of the Anglo-Egyptian attention, the local slavery may have continued: he anthropologist Suzanne Miers states that still in 1923 *"agriculture in Northern Sudan was still based on slave labor"*.[40]

Conclusions – *The end of the Red Sea slave route*

32   Reda Mowafi "Slavery, Slave Trade and Abolition Attempts in Egypt and the Sudan 1820-1882", Lund Studies in international History 14, &ESSELTESTUDIUM, 1981.
33   Harry Verhoeven "Water, civilization and power in Sudan, the political economy of Military-Islamist State Building, African Studies, Cambridge University Press , 2015" the Dongola and Shendi communities were forced to increase their agricultural outputs and all this brought to a massive depopulation of rural areas; Danagla and Ja'aliyyin tribes on the contrary profited by the labor intensive agriculture and the Shaiggiyya tribe became the Turkish taxes collector.
[34]One quantar was 45 kg (Egypt)
[35]Endre Stiansen, Michael Kevane, "Kordofan invaded: peripheral incorporation and social transformation in Islamic Africa"Brill, 1998
36   One quantar was 45 kg (Egypt)
37   Endre Stiansen, Michael Kevane, "Kordofan invaded: peripheral incorporation and social transformation in Islamic Africa", Brill, 1998
38   Following the French invasion in Chad, 1891
39   See P.K. Norris " Cotton production in the Anglo-Egyptian Sudan" Library of Congress, 1934
40   Daniel Pipes, "Chattel slavery in Sudan" 2002.

Egyptian and Sudanese slave trade were the main countries of the Red Sea Market area of slave trade.[41] Since 1800 till 1884, this area provided a sum of 250,000 slaves from the Gulf of Aden, 111,000 from Massawa, 24,000 from Northern Danikil and 107,000 from Suakin. The available datas from West Arabia are of 31,100 slaves imported since 1856 to 1884[42] . During the years after 1884, there is certainly a decrease of the slave trade in this area, but we have not reliable sources on its rhythm. One must consider even that the technological change in transport (especially with steamship) may have influenced the traditional routes of the slave trade, making them different and less traceable than in the past times. Anyway, it is evident that the decrease is due chiefly to the changes in social structure, which destroyed the slavery environment in many countries of the area. Therefore, one can conclude that the first wave of globalization, if – on one hand – boosted the demand for slaves and slave trade, it created also – on the other hand – those social conditions which allowed to overtake this social phenomenon.

Bibliography

1. Charles Issawi "De-Industrialization and Re-Industrialization in the Middle East since 1800", International Journal of Middle East Studies, Vol. 12, No.
2. Daniel Pipes, "Chattel slavery in Sudan" 2002.
3. Endre Stiansen, " Kordofan invaded: peripheral incorporation and social transformation in Islamic Africa", Michael Kevane, Brill, 1998
4. Fage and Roland Oliver "The Cambridge History of Africa".D. Fage and Roland Oliver, Volume V
5. Gabriel Baer, "Slavery in the XIX century Egypt", Journal of African History, 1967
6. Harry Verhoeven "Water, civilization and power in Sudan, the political economy of Military-Islamist State Building"- African Studies, Cambdridge University Press, 2015
7. Justin A. McCarthy, "Nineteenth-Century Egyptian Population", Middle Eastern Studies, Vol. 12, No. 3, Special Issue on the Middle Eastern Economy, Taylor & Francis. 1976
8. Mahmood Mamdani "Saviors and Survivors : Darfur, Politics, and the War on Terror", 2010 Three Rivers Press
9. Paul Tiyambe Zeleza, "A Modern Economic History of Africa: The nineteenth century" figures in table by Roger Owen (1969)
10. Ralph A. Austen, "The 19th century Islamic Slave Trade from East Africa (Swahili and Red Sea Coasts): A Tentative Census". 2008.
11. P. Dunn, JR. " Cotton in Egypt, " National Cotton Council of America 1948

---

41 The Red Sea Market's centers were : (from the North to the South) Suakin, Massawa, Norther Danikil, Gulf of Aden)
42 Ralph A. Austen, "The 19th century Islamic Slave Trade from East Africa (Swahili and Red Sea Coasts): A Tentative Census", University of Chicago Published online: 13 Jun 2008.

12. Reda Mowafi "Slavery, Slave Trade and Abolition Attempts in Egypt and the Sudan 1820-1882", Lund Studies in international History 14, &ESSELTESTUDIUM, 1981
13. Suzanne Miers, "Slavery in the Twentieth Century: the evolution of a global problem" 2003
14. Norris, P.K." Cotton production in the Anglo-Egyptian Sudan" Library of Congress, 1934
15. Tariq M. Yousef, "Egypt's growth performance under economic liberalism: a reassessment with new GDP estimates 1886–1945" Georgetown University, Washington, D.C, Review of Income and Wealth Series 48, Number 4, 2002
16. Zvi Yehuda Hershlag "Introduction to the Modern Economic History of the Middle East", E.J. Brill, Leiden, 1964

YOUR KNOWLEDGE HAS VALUE

- We will publish your bachelor's and master's thesis, essays and papers

- Your own eBook and book - sold worldwide in all relevant shops

- Earn money with each sale

Upload your text at www.GRIN.com
and publish for free